A Home in the Coral Reef

By Christine Taylor-Butler

Children's Press®
A Division of Scholastic Inc.
New York Toronto London Auckland Sydney
Mexico City New Delhi Hong Kong
Danbury, Connecticut

These content vocabulary word builders are for grades 1–2.
Subject Consultant: Susan Woodward, Professor of Geography, Radford University, Radford, Virginia

Reading Consultant: Cecilia Minden-Cupp, PhD, Former Director of the Language and Literacy Program, Harvard Graduate School of Education, Cambridge, Massachusetts

Photographs © 2007: Dembinsky Photo Assoc./Marilyn & Maris Kazmers: 4 bottom left, 5 bottom left, 7, 9; Images & Stories/Zafer Kizilkaya: 21 bottom; Minden Pictures: cover background (Fred Bavendam), back cover, 1, 4 bottom right, 5 bottom right, 8, 11 (Chris Newbert), cover right inset, 2, 5 top right, 10 (Norbert Wu); Photo Researchers, NY: 23 bottom left (Andrew J. Martinez), cover left inset, 20 top (Fred McConnaughey); Seapics.com: 20 bottom (Hal Beral), 23 top left (Don DeMaria), cover center inset, 15, 17, 19, 23 bottom right, 23 top right (Doug Perrine), 4 top, 16 (Espen Rekdal), 5 top left, 13 (Mark Strickland); Superstock, Inc./age/fotostock: 21 top.

Book Design: Simonsays Design!
Book Production: The Design Lab

Library of Congress Cataloging-in-Publication Data

Taylor-Butler, Christine.
A home in the coral reef / by Christine Taylor-Butler.
   p. cm. — (Scholastic news nonfiction readers)
Includes index.
ISBN-10: 0-516-25344-1
ISBN-13: 978-0-516-25344-2
1. Coral reef ecology—Juvenile literature. I. Title. II. Series.
QH541.5.C7T39 2006
577.7'89—dc22   2006002305

2 3 4 5 6 7 8 9 10 R 16 15 14 13 12 11 10 09 08

CONTENTS

WORD HUNT

Look for these words as you read. They will be in **bold**.

algae
(**al**-gee)

coral reef
(**kor**-uhl **reef**)

corals
(**kor**-ulhz)

4

colonies
(**kol**-uh-neez)

coral polyps
(**kor**-uhl **pol**-ips)

eel
(**eel**)

habitat
(**hab**-uh-tat)

5

What Is This Place?

There is warm, clear water all around you.

Colorful fish dart back and forth. A shark swims above your head. An **eel** slithers into a hole.

Where are we?

An eel is a long, thin fish.
Eels look like snakes.

We're in a **coral reef**!

A coral reef is a type of **habitat**. A habitat is where a plant or animal usually lives.

Coral reefs are found in oceans around the world.

habitat

A coral reef is like an underwater city where thousands of animals live.

Corals are made up of many tiny tube-shaped animals called **coral polyps**. There are more than seven hundred different kinds of coral polyps!

coral polyp

Most of the reef is made up of the skeletons of dead corals.

Corals live in **colonies**, or groups. The colonies attach to hard surfaces on the ocean floor. Colonies come in different sizes, shapes, and colors.

Together, many coral colonies make up a reef.

The coral reef provides shelter for many animals.

Crabs, turtles, and jellyfish live in and around the reef.

This sea turtle is eating sea plants. But some sea turtles eat crabs and jellyfish.

Algae are plants that grow on the coral reef. These plants use sunlight to make food and oxygen for corals.

But too much algae isn't good for the reef. Parrot fish help solve this problem.

algae

Parrot fish use their sharp teeth to scrape algae off the corals.

The coral reef is an exciting place to explore! Take a swim through the clear, blue water. You'll meet this stingray and other amazing animals that live in this habitat!

19

A DAY IN THE LIFE OF AN EEL

How does an eel spend most of its time? An eel hides in holes and cracks in rocky areas of the reef.

What does an eel eat? An eel eats octopus, crabs, and fish, including other eels.

What are an eel's enemies? Other eels and large fish called groupers are an eel's enemies.

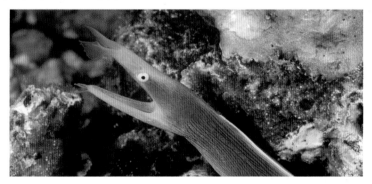

Does an eel have a special survival trick? An eel hides in holes and cracks in rocky areas of the reef.

YOUR NEW WORDS

algae (**al**-gee) simple plants that often grow in moist, or wet, habitats

colonies (**kol**-uh-neez) groups of animals that live in one place

coral polyps (**kor**-uhl **pol**-ips) tiny tube-shaped sea animals that make up corals

coral reef (**kor**-uhl **reef**) an underwater habitat made up of the hardened remains of corals

corals (**kor**-uhlz) ocean animals that are made of polyps and often live in colonies

eel (**eel**) a long, slippery fish with no scales

habitat (**hab**-uh-tat) the place where a plant or animal usually lives

OTHER ANIMALS THAT LIVE IN THE CORAL REEF

pufferfish

shrimp

sponges

urchins

INDEX

FIND OUT MORE

Book:
Nicholson, Sue. *Ocean Explorer*. Lake Mary, Fla.: Tangerine Press, 2001.

Website:
Reef Education Network
http://www.reef.edu.au/

MEET THE AUTHOR:

Christine Taylor-Butler is the author of twenty-four fiction and nonfiction books for children. A graduate of the Massachusetts Institute of Technology, Christine now lives in Kansas City, Missouri, with her husband, two daughters, a pride of mischievous black cats, and two tanks of fish.